Butterflies Up Close

By Sindy McKay

TREASURE BAY

Family Engagement in Reading

Parent's Introduction

Whether your child is a beginning reader, a reluctant reader, or an eager reader, this book offers a fun and easy way to encourage and help your child in reading.

Developed with reading education specialists, **We Both Read** books invite you and your child to take turns reading aloud. You read the left-hand pages of the book, and your child reads the right-hand pages—which have been written at one of six early reading levels. The result is a wonderful new reading experience and faster reading development!

You may find it helpful to read the entire book aloud yourself the first time, then invite your child to participate the second time. As you read, try to make the story come alive by reading with expression. This will help to model good fluency. It will also be helpful to stop at various points to discuss what you are reading. This will help increase your child's understanding of what is being read.

In some books, a few challenging words are introduced in the parent's text, distinguished with **bold** lettering. Pointing out and discussing these words can help to build your child's reading vocabulary. If your child is a beginning reader, it may be helpful to run a finger under the text as each of you reads. Please also notice that a "talking parent" ⊙ icon precedes the parent's text, and a "talking child" ⊙ icon precedes the child's text.

If your child struggles with a word, you can encourage "sounding it out," but keep in mind that not all words can be sounded out. Your child might pick up clues about a word from the picture, other words in the sentence, or any rhyming patterns. If your child struggles with a word for more than five seconds, it is usually best to simply say the word.

Most of all, remember to praise your child's efforts and keep the reading fun. At the end of the book, there is a glossary of words, as well as some questions you can discuss. Rereading this book multiple times may also be helpful for your child.

Try to keep the tips above in mind as you read together, but don't worry about doing everything right. Simply sharing the enjoyment of reading together will increase your child's reading skills and help to start your child off on a lifetime of reading enjoyment!

Butterflies Up Close

A We Both Read Book
Level 1–2
Guided Reading: Level H

With special thanks to
Christopher Grinter
Collection Manager of Entomology,
California Academy of Sciences,
for his advice on the material in this book

Use of photographs provided by iStock, Dreamstime, FotoSearch, and Depositphotos.

We Both Read® is a registered trademark of Treasure Bay, Inc.

Published by Treasure Bay, Inc.
P.O. Box 119
Novato, CA 94948 USA

Printed in Malaysia

Library of Congress Catalog Card Number: 2018954234

ISBN: 978-1-60115-356-2

Visit us online at WeBothRead.com

PR-11-18

TABLE OF CONTENTS

Royal Assyrian

Southern white admiral

Orange, blue, yellow, red, purple. **Butterflies** display some of the most striking colors in nature, and there are **thousands** of different butterfly species, each with a special pattern of colors on its wings. If you look at butterfly wings, you might notice that their colors seem to shimmer in the sunlight. Do you know why the colors shimmer like this?

Red-spotted admiral

Painted jezebel

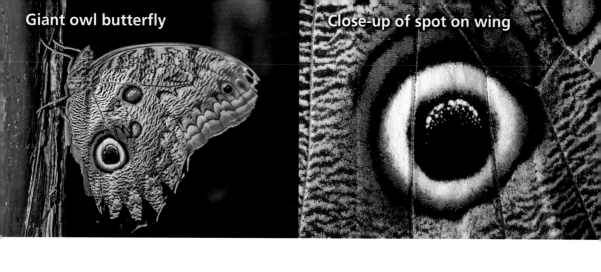

Giant owl butterfly

Close-up of spot on wing

Butterflies have four wings. All four wings have **thousands** of tiny scales on them.

Extreme close-up of scales on wing

3

Blue morpho butterfly

There are multiple layers of these tiny scales on each wing. When light passes through the layers, it is reflected many times over, and that helps to create iridescent colors that seem to shimmer and glow.

4

The scales are very small and hard to see. When the scales fall off, they look more like dust than like scales.

Tiger swallowtail butterfly

Forewing

Hindwing

Thorax

Antennae

Head and eyes

Proboscis

Abdomen

Six legs

Butterflies are insects that have large wings for flight. All insects have three body parts—the head, the thorax, and the abdomen. They all have six jointed legs, two antennae (an-TEN-ee), and eyes. Insects do not have bones; they have an **exoskeleton** (ek-so-SKEL-uh-tin).

Pipevine swallowtail

We have a hard skeleton on the *inside* of our body. An **exoskeleton** is a hard cover on the *outside* of a body. The butterfly's exoskeleton helps to protect it.

Chinese violet cress

Zigzag flat

Leopard lacewing eggs and caterpillars

Did you know that there are no baby butterflies?

A butterfly starts out as an egg, which hatches into a caterpillar. Once the caterpillar is fully **grown**, it forms itself into a **chrysalis** (KRIS-uh-lis). Inside the chrysalis, the caterpillar transforms.

Banded wooly bear caterpillar

Swallowtail caterpillar

Life Cycle of a Monarch Butterfly

Adult

Chrysalis

Egg

Older caterpillar

Young caterpillar

When the **chrysalis** opens, a full-**grown** butterfly comes out. That is why you will never see a baby butterfly!

Butterfly eggs come in many shapes, sizes, and colors. Some butterflies lay only one egg at a time, while some lay their eggs in small clusters. Others lay hundreds of eggs on one **leaf**. The photos on these two pages are close-up views of different butterfly eggs.

You may find butterfly eggs on a **leaf** in your garden. If you do, you may want to check them every day. Most eggs hatch in three to seven days.

Egg and newly hatched caterpillar

When an egg hatches, a **caterpillar** emerges. Caterpillars are like eating machines! Their only job is to grow. They grow so fast that they must shed their skin, or *molt*, **often** as they grow.

Atlas caterpillar that is molting

Butterfly laying eggs

A mother butterfly **often** lays her eggs on a leaf that the **caterpillar** likes to eat. The caterpillar can eat the leaf as soon as it hatches.

Monarch caterpillar

Monarch caterpillar shedding its skin as it transforms into a chrysalis

Monarch chrysalis

Once a caterpillar is finished growing, it sheds its skin, or molts, one last time to reveal the chrysalis layer beneath. The chrysalis layer is soft at first but soon hardens into a firm shell. Inside this shell, the caterpillar begins to **change**.

Monarch butterfly

Its mouth **changes** into something more like a straw. Wings form so it can fly. It takes 9 to 14 days for all the changes to happen.

Monarch emerging from chrysalis

Once the change, or metamorphosis (met-uh-MORE-fuh-sis), has happened, the butterfly is ready to come out of its shell. The chrysalis cracks and the butterfly wriggles out, damp and crumpled.

The butterfly rests for a bit. Then it starts to flap its wings. It takes some time, but soon it flies away.

Proboscis (pruh-BAH-sis)

Great spangled fritillary butterfly

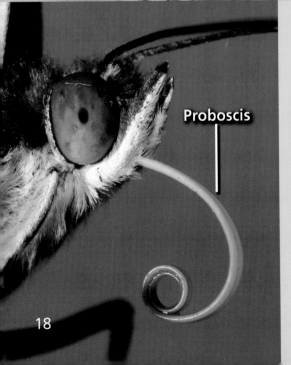

Proboscis

Newly developed butterflies spend their days eating, flying, and resting. When the butterfly was a caterpillar, it could chew on a leaf. But butterflies don't have mouths that can chew. Instead they have a **proboscis** (pruh-BAH-sis). The **proboscis** is like a straw that lets them sip **liquids**.

Butterflies use their **proboscis** to sip nectar from flowers. Nectar is a sweet **liquid** inside flowers that butterflies and bees love to drink.

Yellow vein lancer

The proboscis stays curled up under the butterfly's chin as it flies around the garden. When the butterfly finds the right flower, it uncurls its proboscis and uses it to sip the flower's nectar. While sipping the nectar, the butterfly gets covered in a powdery substance from the flower, called **pollen**.

Longwing butterfly

Postman butterfly

Proboscis with
yellow pollen on it

The butterfly then flies off, and some of the **pollen** drops on the next flower. Flowers need pollen to make seeds that will grow into new flowers. That is one reason people like to have butterflies in their garden.

Blue morphos

Butterflies spend much of their time flying, but they can fly only when the temperature is just right. If a butterfly gets too cold, it finds a warm spot to spread its wings and soak up the sun. This is called *basking*.

Tortoiseshell butterfly basking on a rock

If a butterfly gets too hot, it looks for shade. On a hot day, you may see one resting under a leaf. You may also see butterflies in a puddle. They are not doing this to cool off. They are having a drink.

Orange albatross butterflies that are "puddling"

Monarch butterfly

If butterflies can't find the right temperature or enough food, they may have to travel—or **migrate**—to a new location. The new location may be just around the corner, but for some butterflies, like **monarchs**, it may be a different country!

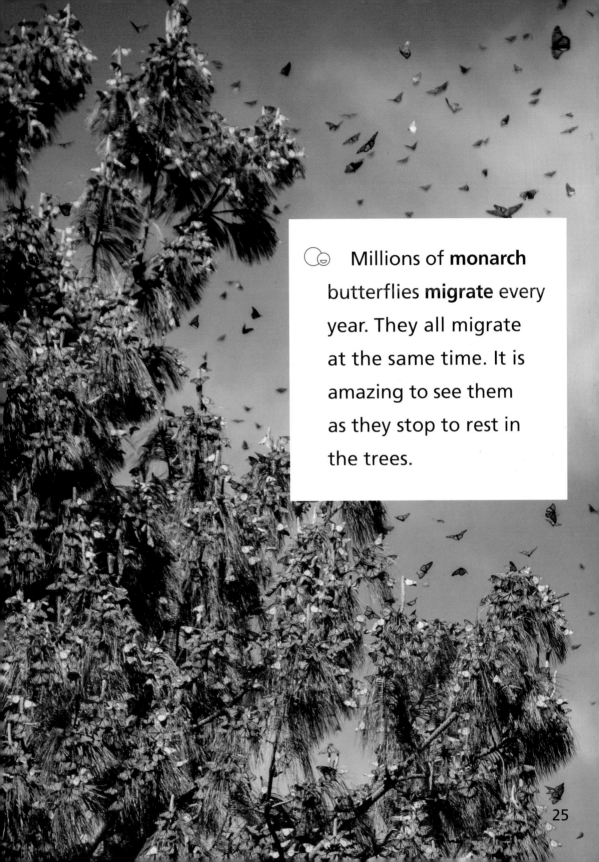

Millions of **monarch** butterflies **migrate** every year. They all migrate at the same time. It is amazing to see them as they stop to rest in the trees.

Rosy maple moth

Zygaenidae moth

Nine-spotted moth

Oleander hawk moth

Emperor moth

Garden tiger moth

These lovely creatures look a lot like butterflies, but don't be fooled—these are moths! All moths are in the same order of insects as butterflies, called *Lepidoptera* (leh-pih-DOP-ter-uh). Lepidoptera means "scaly wings."

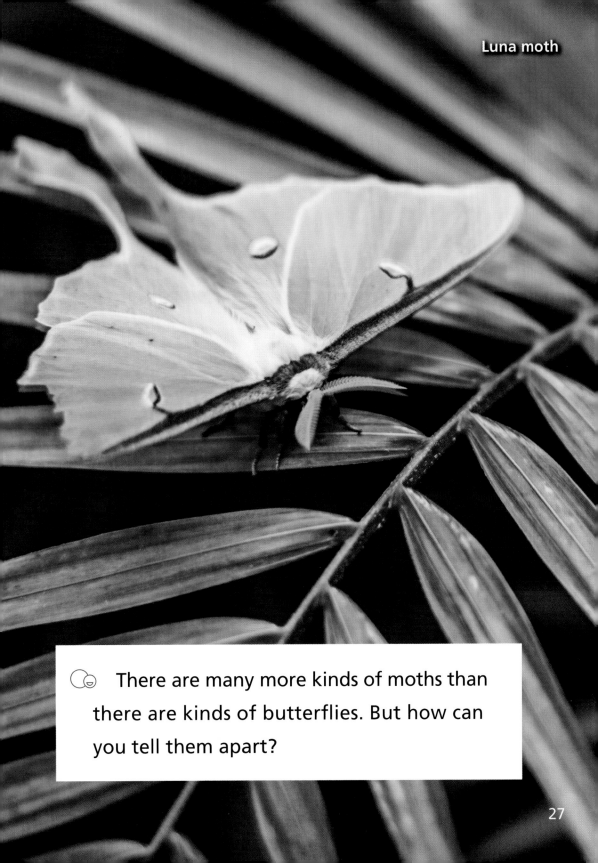

There are many more kinds of moths than there are kinds of butterflies. But how can you tell them apart?

One way to tell them apart is to look closely at their antennae. A butterfly's antennae usually have a bulb on the end. Most moth antennae are fuzzy or feathery.

Moth antennae

Atala butterfly resting

When a butterfly rests, it holds its wings up. When a moth rests, it lays its wings flat. Most butterflies fly when the sun is out. Most moths fly at night.

Small emperor moth

Bird eating caterpillar

Humans aren't the only species that appreciate Lepidoptera (leh-pih-DOP-tuh-ruh). Several animals depend on these insects for food, so many butterflies, moths, and caterpillars have developed unique ways to keep from being eaten by **predators**.

Iguana eating insect

Merveille du jour moth

Cracker butterfly

Many butterflies, moths, and caterpillars blend in with the plants around them. This makes them hard to see. It helps them hide from the **predators**.

Eye-hawk moth caterpillar (Hint: It looks just like a leaf, and it is in the middle of the photo.)

Poplar grey moth

31

Cinnabar caterpillars (toxic to eat)

**Saddleback caterpillar
(venomous spines)**

Some Lepidoptera don't worry about being seen by predators. These insects are poisonous—or **toxic**—and the predators that eat them **often** get very sick or even die. Some caterpillars keep predators away with spines or hairs that can sting with painful venom.

Spotted blue crow butterfly

The wings of **toxic** butterflies are **often** made up of very bold, shimmery colors. This tells predators to stay away!

Postman butterfly

Tiger heliconian butterfly

Pipevine swallowtail (toxic)

Spicebush swallowtail (not toxic)

Mimicry is another tool some butterflies use to avoid being someone's dinner. **Mimicry** is when a species of animal is safer by looking very similar to another animal or even a plant. For example, if a tasty butterfly looks very similar to a poisonous species, predators probably won't eat it.

Monarch butterfly (toxic)

Viceroy butterfly (not toxic)

Giant owl butterfly

Some butterflies have wings that **mimic** the eyes of an owl. Some caterpillars look like snakes. Another caterpillar looks like bird poop!

Spicebush swallowtail caterpillar

Golden birdwing butterfly

Western pygmy blue butterfly

← actual size

There are over 17,000 different varieties of butterflies around the world—about 750 in the United States alone! The largest known butterfly is the Queen Alexandra's birdwing. One of the smallest is the western pygmy blue.

Banded peacock, known for speed

Some butterflies can fly very fast. They do not want to be a meal for a predator! Toxic butterflies do not have to fly fast. Predators do not chase them.

Zebra butterflies, toxic and known for slow, graceful flying

Neglected eighty-eight butterfly

Many butterfly varieties have unusual markings and traits. The neglected eighty-eight butterfly appears to have numbers on its wings. The Greta oto butterfly seems to have wings of glass. It's pretty obvious where the dead leaf butterfly got its name!

Greta oto or glasswing butterfly

Orange oakleaf or dead leaf butterfly

Butterflies can be found all over the world. Some are very rare. Some are big. Some are small. And some need our help.

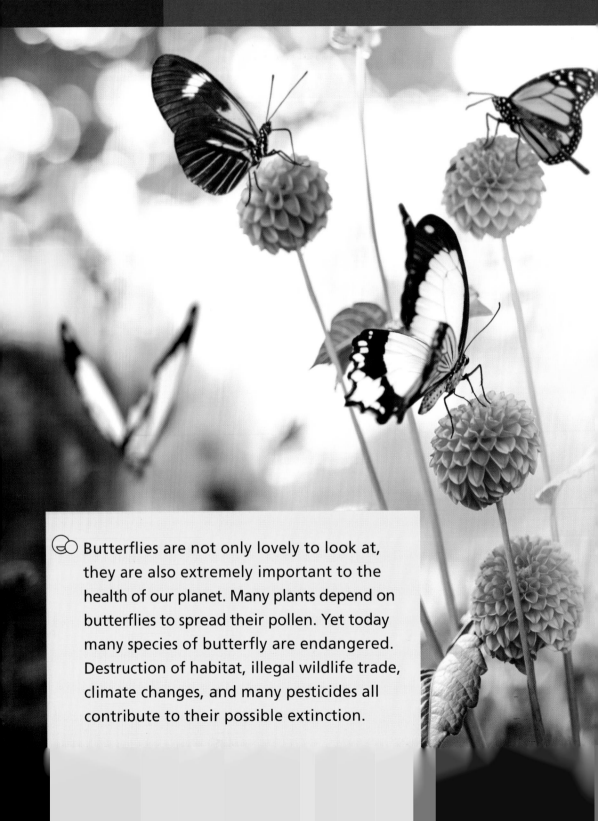

Butterflies are not only lovely to look at, they are also extremely important to the health of our planet. Many plants depend on butterflies to spread their pollen. Yet today many species of butterfly are endangered. Destruction of habitat, illegal wildlife trade, climate changes, and many pesticides all contribute to their possible extinction.

But you can help! Find out what kinds of plants and flowers the caterpillars and butterflies in your area like. Then ask if you can plant some in your garden. Soon you may see beautiful butterflies as they flit from flower to flower.

Glossary

chrysalis (KRIS-uh-lis)
a hard case in which a caterpillar transforms into a butterfly

iridescent
shining with bright colors that seem to shimmer or change with movement

pollen
the very fine dust produced by flowers, which is carried to other flowers and lets them produce seeds

predator
an animal that eats other animals

proboscis (pruh-BAH-sis)
a straw-like tube that lets a butterfly sip nectar from flowers

toxic
poisonous

Questions to Ask after Reading

Add to the benefits of reading this book by discussing answers to these questions. Also consider discussing a few of your own questions.

1 Have you ever seen a butterfly?
Do you remember where you saw it?
What time of year was it?

2 Why do you think gardeners love butterflies but do not like caterpillars?

3 Can you think of anything else in nature that has a shimmering or iridescent quality?

4 Can you think of any other animals that use poison to ward off predators?

5 What are some reasons butterflies might migrate?

If you liked **Butterflies Up Close,** here are some other We Both Read® books you are sure to enjoy! You can see all the We Both Read books that are available at WeBothRead.com.

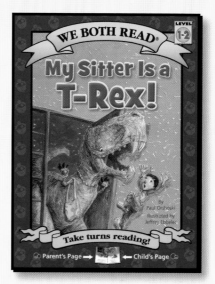